A JOURNA

MW01413453

BE *Well!*

Feeling Good • Struggling Well • Functioning Effectively

P E R M A H

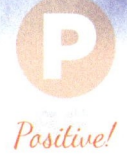

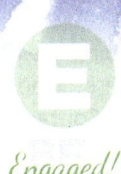

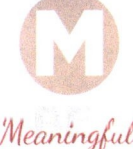

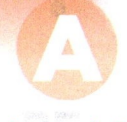

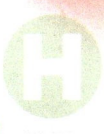

Positive! Engaged! Relational! Meaningful! Accomplished! Healthy!

Diane M. Rogers

Copyright © MMXXIII by Diane M. Rogers

All rights reserved. This book or any portion thereof may not be reproduced or used in any manner whatsoever without the express written permission of the author, except for the use of brief quotations in a book review.

Printed in the United States of America

First Printing, 2023

ISBN: 978-1-953640-28-4 (paperback)

A Page Beyond
11650 Olio Road
Suite 1000 #392
Fishers, IN 46037
www.APageBeyond.com

a page beyond

Ordering Information:
Special discounts are available on quantity purchases by corporations, associations, and others who purchase directly from the author. Contact diane@contagiouschange.com for details.

This journal belongs to

_____

Throughout this journey, I will take conscious and intentional actions coupled with discovery and reflection to create change within myself.

I will take intentional steps to BE well.

**Feeling Good
Struggling Well
Functioning Effectively**

BE Positive
Showing up positively

BE Engaged
Leveraging our strengths

BE Relational
Cultivating Connection

BE Meaningful
Making a Difference

BE Accomplished
Learning from doing

BE Healthy
Moving, Resting & Eating

Source: Seligman, Martin, E. P., *Flourish; A Visionary New Understanding of Happiness and Well-Being*, New York, Atria Paperback, 2011

**Feeling Good
Struggling Well
Functioning Effectively**

What **door** would you like this journey to open for you?

You are beginning a journey toward wellBEING.

On this page, **acknowledge yourself** for showing up and choosing to discover the magnificence within yourself.

Week 1: BE Well

> **Start where you are at.
> Use what you have.
> Do what you can.**
> *-Arthur Ashe*

Remind yourself that while you are at the beginning of your journey toward wellBEING, you are not starting from zero.

Fill this page with the **A**bility, **M**otivation, **and P**ractices you already possess that will **AMP**lify a healthier version of yourself.

Week 2: BE Well

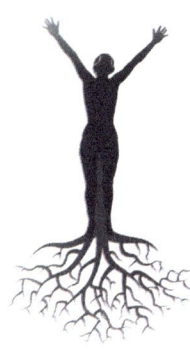

BEING healthy requires exercising healthy habits: moving, eating, sleeping, and drinking.

Use this page to **acknowledge yourself** for the healthy habits in your routine and set goals for the habits you'd like to establish this year.

Week 3: BE Healthy

My habits: **My goals:**

BE a **rockstar** when it comes to your health. Imagine how you can use music as part of your journey toward wellBEING.

Week 4: BE Healthy

As you have set your intentions on BEING healthy... what has **surprised** you the most?

Reflect on how your perspective has changed since beginning this journey.

Week 5: BE Healthy

Pause. Breathe. Repeat.

Focusing on BEING healthy includes your mental health.

Take a moment to breathe in positive energy and note what you experience.

Week 6: BE Healthy

What is a play activity you enjoyed as a child? How can you incorporate aspects of **play** into your healthy lifestyle today?

Week 7: BE Healthy

> **A mind once stretched by a new idea never regains its original dimension.**
> *- Oliver Wendell Holmes*

How has your mindset shifted as you've focused your intentions on **BEING healthy**?

Week 8: BE Healthy

Healthy

Week 9: BE Positive

With each day and with each experience, you have a choice as to how you show up. Reflect on a time when you consciously chose to **BE positive**.

How did that change your experience?

Search for magnificence everywhere you go.

Fill this page with as many examples, big or small, that you can find this week.

Week 10: BE Positive

Positive!

Choose to purposefully bring **positive energy** into your way of BEING.

On this page, fill in the positive actions you will take on purpose this week.

Week 11: BE Positive

I will BE joyful by...

I will BE loving by...

I will BE grateful by...

I will BE awesome by...

How will you fill the **canvas of your life** with positive energy?

Week 12: BE Positive

Positive!

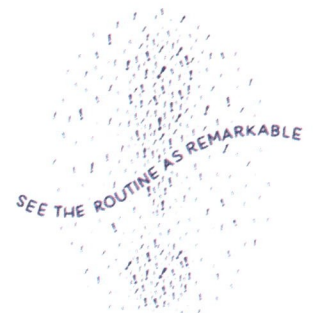

When you shift your mindset and see the elements of your daily routine as **remarkable**, you are BEING positive.

On this page, reflect on one or more aspects of your routine that are remarkable.

Week 13: BE Positive

Practice **gratitude**. Shift your energy and observations to notice the good.

On this page, write 10 things you are grateful for today.

Week 14: BE Positive

1.

2.

3.

4.

5.

6.

7.

8.

9.

10.

What is filling your bucket?

Week 15: BE Positive

Positive!

What acknowledgement do you wish to offer yourself?

Week 16: BE Positive

Positive!

What **positive emotions** are you experiencing in choosing how you wish to show up?

Week 17: BE Positive

Positive!

BE engaged by leveraging your strengths.

On this page, identify as many of your **personal strengths** as you can.

Week 18: BE Engaged

Engaged!

How will you shift your mindset to activate your on-purpose awareness to discover the **best in others**?

What are you noticing in doing so?

Week 19: BE Engaged

Engaged!

The best of you comes from within.

What **essence** of your best self will you choose to bring forward further today?

Week 20: BE Engaged

Engaged!

Strengths

What **strengths** are you noticing in others?

Week 21: BE Engaged

Engaged!

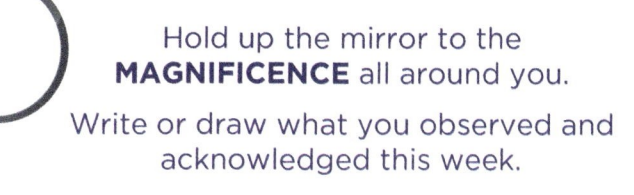

Hold up the mirror to the **MAGNIFICENCE** all around you.

Write or draw what you observed and acknowledged this week.

Week 22: BE Engaged

Engaged!

actions attitudes behaviors

Week 23: BE Engaged

Take note of the **actions, attitudes, and behaviors** you are noticing in others.

actions

attitudes

behaviors

Engaged!

Everyone is a **star**. Help them shine!

What are you shining a light on for others to see their magnificence?

Week 24: BE Engaged

Engaged!

Listen with the intention to **uncover the 'who'** - not the what - in each situation.

What magnificence is unfolding when you adopt this intention?

Week 25: BE Engaged

Engaged!

Remind others of their **best selves**.
For each strength below, identify a person who embodies this quality.

Week 26: BE Engaged

- teamwork:
- humor:
- creativity:
- kindness:
- fairness:
- bravery:
- honesty:
- leadership:

Engaged!

In consciously and intentionally showing up as your **best self**, and discovering the best in others, what is lighting you up?

Week 27: BE Engaged

Engaged!

Daily conversation is at the heart of building relationships.

What pleasant conversations will you **consciously and intentionally** bring into your day?

Week 28: BE Relational

Relational!

Week 29: BE Relational

We are more **alike** than we are **unalike**.

On this page, pick 2 people in your life and write down all of the characteristics they both share.

Relational!

a **BE Community Builder!**

Week 30: BE Relational

Having a sense of belonging within a community is essential to BEING well.

This week, consciously and intentionally invite others in.

How will you build your **community**?

Relational!

Magnificence is found in individuals all around you.

On this page, share a **MAGNIFICENT** story that you have seen or heard.

Week 31: BE Relational

Relational!

When you turn your observer on to discover the best in others, you activate your superpower to make people **un-invisible**.

On this page, share how you made people un-invisible this week.

Week 32: BE Relational

Relational!

Leave footprints that others will want to follow.

On each footprint, acknowledge yourself for an action or quality that would inspire others to **follow your lead**.

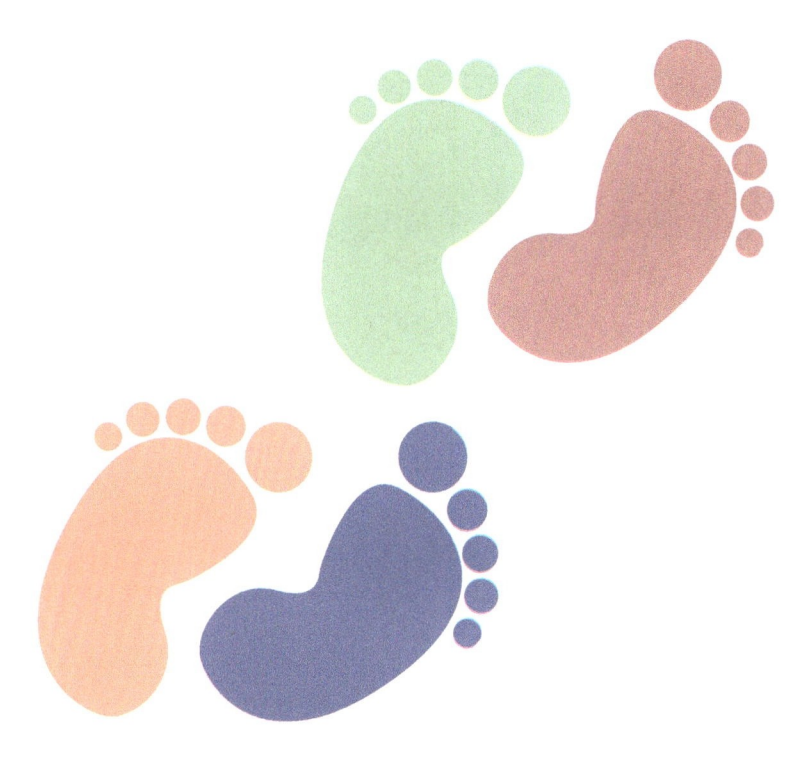

Week 33: BE Relational

Relational!

> **Remind people who they are instead of just complimenting them on what they've done.**
> — *Oliver Wendell Holmes*

Identify **positive actions** (what) you noticed in others; and imagine what **intrinsic qualities** (who) were present to prompt that action.

How will you uncover the 'who,' translating what you noticed into an acknowledgement?

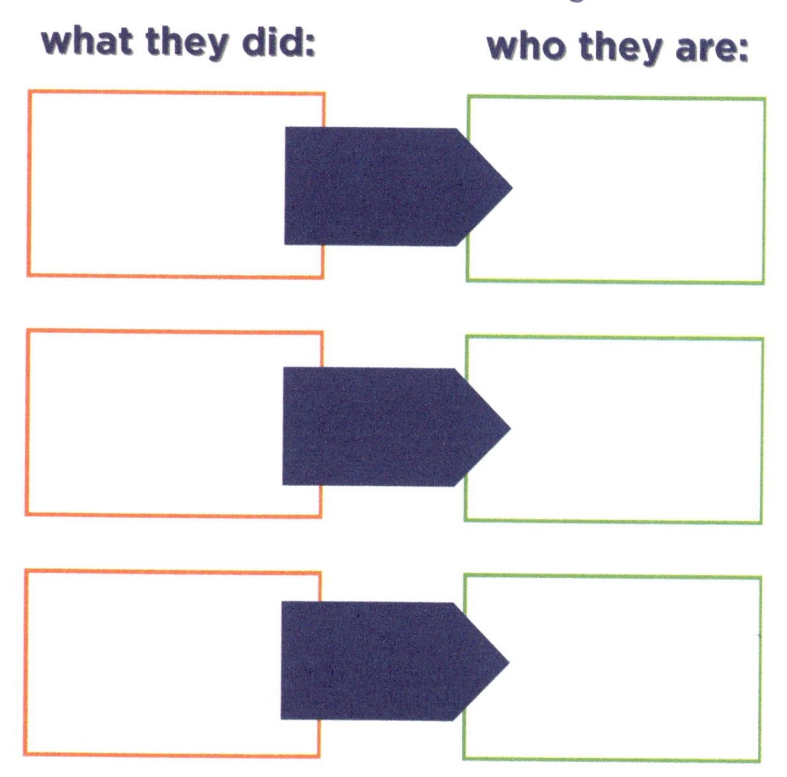

Week 34: BE Relational

what they did:	who they are:
	→
	→
	→

Relational!

Everyone wants to feel like they belong. Create conversations where individuals feel **cared for and valued**.

With whom will you create a conversation to foster a sense of belonging?

Week 35: BE Relational

Relational!

BE Meaningful!

Connect meaning to purpose.

What purposeful intention will bring **meaningfulness** into your day?

Week 36: BE Meaningful

yes you can

How you show up matters.
Bring the best of you to the best of others.

On this page, identify the ways that you chose 'yes' to **make a difference**.

Week 37: BE Meaningful

Meaningful!

> **Never doubt that a small group of thoughtful, committed citizens can change the world. Indeed it is the only thing that ever has.**
> *- Margret Mead*

Never doubt your capacity to change A world.

Write a **mantra for yourself** that you will use to remind you of your capacity to change A world.

Week 38: BE Meaningful

Meaningful!

"Everyone has the capacity to change a world."

BEING Meaningful changes worlds - yours included.

What elements of wellBEING are amplified when you intentionally **change A world**?

P Positive!
E Engaged!
R Relational!
M Meaningful!
A Accomplished!
H Healthy!

Week 39: BE Meaningful

Meaningful!

There is no time like **NOW** to create a reflective practice.

Pause & Reflect

How has showing up as your best self made a difference this week?

Week 40: BE Meaningful

Meaningful!

Be kind to yourself.

Fill this page with ways you will show yourself **kindness** this week.

Week 41: BE Meaningful

Something I can do for myself is...

Something I can say to myself is...

I can recharge by...

I can show gratitude for myself by...

Meaningful!

How you show up is how they show up.

How will you choose to show up this week?

Week 42: BE Meaningful

Meaningful!

1 2 3 Values

Where do you see the presence of your **values**?

Week 43: BE Meaningful

Meaningful!

BE Accomplished!

When you set an intention to BE accomplished, you set forth to **learn from DOING**.

What are you learning this week?

Week 44: BE Accomplished

> **I did then what I knew how to do. Now that I know better, I do better.**
> — Maya Angelou

Take a moment to reflect on your life.

What is something that you now **do better** because of what you have learned?

Week 45: BE Accomplished

Accomplished!

Accomplishment is learning through DOING and invites inquiry.

What do you know now?

What did you learn?

What would be different if you had a **do-over**?

Week 46: BE Accomplished

Accomplished!

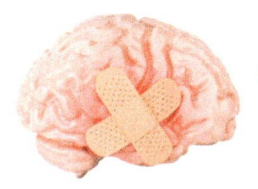

Be perfectly **imperfect**!

Use the shapes below to create a drawing - or several drawings. Allow yourself to be imperfect in your creation.

Week 47: BE Accomplished

Accomplished!

Turn your **'To-Do$_s$'** *into* **'Ta-Das'!**
—M. McQuaid

Week 48: BE Accomplished

Celebrate your **accomplishments**.

On this page, write 5 things that you have achieved this week.

1.

2.

3.

4.

5.

Accomplished!

> **Never underestimate the impact that your mere existence can have on another human being.**
> - Fred Rogers

Week 49: BE Accomplished

Never underestimate **YOU**.

On this page, acknowledge yourself for the positive impact you've had this week.

Oh, and be specific!

Accomplished!

Week 50: BE Accomplished

Knowledge is not enough. BEING well is an evolutionary journey - Learn, Choose, Do, Reflect.

What will you choose to do with the **knowledge** you have gained?

Accomplished!

BE Well!

Feeling Good
Struggling Well
Functioning Effectively

Throughout this journey, how as each element of wellBEING contributed to your wellBEING; Feeling good, Struggling well & functioning effectively?

Week 51: BE Well

P — *Positive!*

E — *Engaged!*

R — *Relational!*

M — *Meaningful!*

A — *Accomplished!*

H — *Healthy!*

BE Well!

Feeling Good
Struggling Well
Functioning Effectively

What door has this journey toward **wellBEING** opened for you?

Week 52: BE Well

Well!

BE Well!

**Feeling Good
Struggling Well
Functioning Effectively**

You dedicated your year to conscious and intentional actions, coupled with discovery and reflection. This process has led you to better understand how BEING healthy, positive, relational, meaningful, and accomplished amplify and elevate your sense of **wellBEING**.

What is next on this journey for you?

Use this page to set new goals to Do, Tweak, and BE as you continue your journey toward BEING well.

P *Positive!* **E** *Engaged!* **R** *Relational!* **M** *Meaningful!* **A** *Accomplished!* **H** *Healthy!*

CONTAGIOUS CHANGE®

Our Calling

To create a contagious change where everyone's magnificence is made un-invisible.

Specializing in bringing a **strengths-based, appreciative coaching approach** to performance and experience, Contagious Change works with clients to tailor **leadership development and staff engagement programs that drive positive and productive change** to achieve new levels of potential through **discovering the MAGNIFICENCE within each individual.**

Want to learn more about how your organization can benefit from Contagious Change's offerings? Visit contagiouschange.com.

About Diane Rogers

Diane Rogers is the founder and CEO of Contagious Change®, LLC and developer of The hArt of Medicine® series of programs – Leading hArtfully®, Engaging the hArt® & Magnifying Magnificence. Our strengths-based, appreciative programs are designed to equip, engage, and encourage individuals to BE their best – to see their MAGNIFICENCE, and to bring the best of themselves to the best of others.

CONTAGIOUS CHANGE®

Contagious Change offers a variety of programs designed to make each individual's magnificence un-invisible.

LEADERSHIP DEVELOPMENT

Equips leaders with practices, mindsets and frameworks to lead with a strengths-based, appreciative, coaching approach

TEAM ENGAGEMENT & EXPERIENCE

Orients & equips individuals with specific actions, attitudes & behaviors, together with intrinsic strengths to create therapeutic relationships

PHYSICIAN COACHING

Leverages the principles and practices of positive psychology, the science of wellBEING and the art & heart of meaningful discovery to invite intentional action through a strengths-based, coaching approach

SIGNATURE PROGRAMS

The hArt of Medicine®
Leading hArtfully®
Engaging the hArt™
Magnificent Impressions™
Holding Up the Mirror™

ACKNOWLEDGEMENTS

The BE Well Journal is based on the research and work of Martin E. P. Seligman, PhD – Best-selling author, & Director of the Penn Positive Psychology Center and Zellerbach Family Professor of Psychology, University of Pennsylvania. His definition of WellBEING and actionable construct (PERMA) is outlined in his book *Flourish: A Visionary New Understanding of Happiness and Well-being.*

Other thought leaders, including Michelle McQuaid, PhD - Co-creator of the PERMAH Workplace Survey & Founder of The Wellbeing Lab, and Louis Alloro, MAPP – Champion of Change & Co-Creator of The WellBEING Lab programs have contributed directly to my ever-expanding knowledge and understanding of what it is to BE Well and positively influenced the lens through which wellBEING is presented in this Journal.

—

The magic of this book is made possible by two individuals whose artistry and creative energy brought this to life.

Through their extraordinary ability to translate concepts into tangible content, coupled with a bold and beautiful presentation and style, they each bring to life - vividly and in full color - what it is to BE well.

With gobs of gratitude -
Thank you...

Lauren Fassl, Chief Creative Connector

Shannon Slocum, Artistic Magician